A Garden in Liberty

Dan Hutcherson

ISBN-13: 978-0-9984452-5-0

Cover design by YeMi L. Hutcherson

This book is dedicated to
my grandparents.

Table of Contents

Preface

It all started in 2012 on an overseas trip with my wife. I realized I was a Christian, though the full extent didn't sink in until many years later. I also returned home that summer with a phrase stuck in my head: "You cannot be given rights you already have." In hindsight, these events started a search for truth.

I was drawn to learn more about natural rights, the role of government, and basic economic principles. There was an insatiable desire to consume any book, podcast, or commentary that discussed liberty. All the while, I was evaluating my discoveries against the stories of my childhood, particularly the Fall of Man. I didn't know what I was looking for, but I found a personal God.

* * *

My journey resulted in an appreciation for the righteous traditions of Western civilization. I saw how God labored to restore the economic, political, and religious realms. No school of thought influenced me more than the Austrian school of economics. But any discipline of reason can only manifest through a moral population.

I began to notice the real conflict is spiritual, embedded in the nature of man. There is a battle for the human soul. The forces of good and evil became apparent, and I experienced conflict within myself. However, a silent voice guided me through the fog of war, and I came out as a living testimony to an eternal truth.

* * *

This book and its companion, *A Garden in Hedon*, are a product of my spiritual journey. I spent years texting little revelations to myself, then even more time distilling "my notes" into these books. I recognize the content to be groundbreaking but also mere reality around me. As such, credit must go where it's due.

I take full credit for the mistakes herein but defer all glory to God for any valid insight. He made the world with unimaginable depth and beauty. The influence of my late grandfather, Sun Moon, can also be seen throughout. His book, *Exposition of the Divine Principle*, provided the lens to unlock providential history.

* * *

This book contains twenty-one chapters, which are listed in alphabetical order. There is no intentional title arrangement other than placing the crosswalk first.

Each chapter was originally created as a two-slide presentation. The title slide provided a basic introduction, while the second slide wrapped content between its own introduction and conclusion. I have kept this structure intact throughout this book.

The section headings are what used to be bullets and sub-bullets within the presentation. They showcase a direct mapping between the family and nation. These parallels are maintained through the use of a vertical bar.

* * *

I wrote this skeletal book to carry out my personal responsibility. I desire only to record these self-evident truths, and I pray my observations require minimal correction by posterity.

Let your conscience be your guide.

Dan Hutcherson
Child of God

A Garden in Liberty

A Divine Crosswalk

The Book of Genesis contains a divine crosswalk.

* * *

The model of the family extends into a free market.

God develops Creation | Invisible hand develops environment

Every element of Creation comes from God's act of production.
All natural laws, scientific laws, the standard for morality, and all relationships under the invisible hand stem from God (Genesis 1).

True Adam invests love | Producer invests wealth

A True Adam extends God's breath of life (Genesis 2:7) into his spouse through love, regardless of the verbal, sexual, or other form it takes.
This is like a producer orienting operations around providing his wealth to the consumer via a product or service.

True Eve returns beauty | Consumer returns revenue

A True Eve, having received God's love from True Adam, naturally reciprocates love through beauty.
This is like a sincere consumer wants to provide honest money back to the producer as revenue.
The money itself is merely a representation of the producer's need that is being satisfied by the consumer.

Sex continues life | Transaction continues life

The exchange of love, particularly sexual, spawns life by creating children in what now is a family.

This is like how economic transactions can spawn new actors in an expansion of the free market.

Family shares lineage | Free market shares lineage

The entire family tree and free market share the same central, originating root.
It's the ancestral blood that is traced back to God, our Heavenly Father.

Lucifer remains servant | Government remains servant

Lucifer and the institutions of man, like government, naturally serve out their intended purpose.
There is harmony because every action serves not just an individual but also a collective purpose.

* * *

God's will throughout human history has been to share love within a family and free market. It really is that simple.

Act of Marriage

The universe revolves around sex, for better or worse. The act of marriage has the power over literal life (a baby) and death (Genesis 2:17) like in the Fall of Man. You can forget trying to control State power when you aren't even responsible over your own sexual desires.

* * *

A divine perspective on sex is crucial to living in a free society.

Sexual relationship I Economic transaction

The sexual and economic relationship is the battle line between good and evil.

Sperm I Product/service

The sperm brings life itself, and this seed of production contains the potential for a son or daughter.
This is like a product or service has the potential to spawn future producers or consumers.

Egg I Need

Just like God's breath brought life to dust (Genesis 2:7), the producer's seed brings life to the egg when two become one (Genesis 2:24).
This is like a product or service satisfying the consumer's need, which provides the basis for downstream actors.

Marriages expand love I Markets expand wealth

A strong marriage and market culture bears good fruit (Matthew 7:15-20), particularly over the long run.

Survival of the fittest | Survival of the fittest

Most sperm, like ideas for a product or service, are never brought to market.
Millions start the journey but only one sperm combines with an egg.
It's the survival of the fittest where those that survive make life bloom.

Birth of child | Birth of actor

The process of coming to term or delivering a new actor is a labor of love.
A child opens the door for parents and a parental market to experience a new love.

Death (miscarriage) | Death (discontinued)

Physical death is guaranteed and can occur in the womb, at a ripe old age, or anywhere in between.
This is like a product or service being discontinued during development, after market decline, or in unexpected bankruptcy.
These are natural forms of death, unlike the death that entered as a result of the Fall (Genesis 2:17).

* * *

A society begins to degrade when sexual perversions become accepted. In contrast, a society will flourish when the act of marriage is treasured as sacred.

Body of Christ

Humans are unique compared to all other aspects of Creation. We are given a spirit through His breath of life (Genesis 2:7).

* * *

Each child of God is an individual embodiment of truth (John 14:6), like a cell in the body of Christ (Romans 12:4-5).

Cell -> Individual | Individual -> Nation

Cells make up the human body, like individuals make up the nation. Cells form, mature, and die in an individual, like individuals spawn, live, and die in the nation.

Intelligent design | Natural order

Every cell and individual is interconnected and moves in harmony and order.
God's will is exercised with and through humanity, like a mind over its body.

Bodily systems | Market systems

The individual and nation each have internal systems, both voluntary and involuntary.
The various anatomical systems are like different sectors of an economy.

Digestive/immune/excretory | Materials/security/waste

There are systems that intake foods for digestion, like bringing natural resources or raw materials into production.
There are protective functions like the immune system or the security sector at large.
And there are waste management systems designed to take out the trash.

Energy allocation I Resource allocation

The allocation of energy, like love and the wealth of resources, can change based on the circumstances.
A young body allocates differently than an older one, like areas of growth see additional capital while aging areas begin to fade out.
Parts of the body will even shut down when injured in order to focus on survival, like supply chains can restructure to reallocate resources in a crisis.

Garden of Eden (outside) I Kingdom of Heaven (outside)

The Fall of Man was an act of self-harm for the cells and body.

One family under Satan I One nation under State

Satan exercises his desires with and through humanity, too, but without harmony and order.
Those children most demonic climb the power ladder to control, farm, even murder their brethren through the State.
The misallocation of resources through malinvestment becomes an everyday reality.

Bodily systems I Market systems

All the functions that exist in God's body still exist but they're distorted, like an immune system that attacks rather than protect the body.
The individual and nation is crippled with various ailments, diseases, and cancers that may appear productive but provide no value.

* * *

The entirety of the body of Christ really is just an extension of one man, a True Adam. You'll know where you belong once you have relationship with Him.

Bound by Blood

The distinction between child and servant is in the blood. God created and worked with angels before creating Adam and Eve (Genesis 1:26). This is like a producer creating and working with employees before coming to market. But the producer, like God, has his bride in mind from the start.

* * *

Adam and Eve were not mere animals, like a producer and consumer are categorically distinct from servants.

True Adam/True Eve | Producer/consumer

A True Adam and True Eve are God's children, not servants, so their bond is based on blood.

They become one in marriage, like a producer and consumer becomes a market.

Collective ownership | Collective ownership

A True Adam needs a True Eve (Genesis 2:18); it's only together that a family is created.

This is like the producer and consumer are co-creators, co-owners over the market.

But this relationship is always centered on Adam's seed of production.

Lineage hierarchy | Lineage hierarchy

The children of God receive love and ownership by being in a hierarchy of familial bonds that trace directly back to God.

This is like tracing the ancestry of actors in the free market back to the very first market of origin.

Angels/animals (Lucifer) | Employees/institutions (government)

Each of these groups are servants to their respective owners.

Their labor or skillset is exchanged for some form of payment.

Designed to serve | Designed to serve

Servants are designed by their owners to act in a delegated capacity. There is no intrinsic basis for inheritance or ownership since there's no familial bond.

Meritocratic hierarchy | Meritocratic hierarchy

All servants function within a ladder of competence based on meritocratic values.

Even the highest of servants, like Lucifer, still looks up to the children of God.

They are functionally replaceable whereas children can never be replaced.

Garden of Eden (outside) | Kingdom of Heaven (outside)

Adam and Eve became bound by blood with Satan as a result of the Fall of Man.

Means of production | Means of production

Satan assumes ownership over Adam's seed of production, like the State assumes the means of production.

This corruption of blood negatively impacts every relationship in the economy.

* * *

It's only after the children of God are revealed that Satan can return to his delegated role as Lucifer (Romans 8:19-23). This is like the total elimination of the State is only possible after we're bound by blood with God.

Divide and Conquer

The phrase "divide and conquer" has a negative connotation, but Satan merely distorts a natural process of multiplication.

* * *

In the beginning, there was one God (Genesis 1:1). God created two in His image (Genesis 1:27), then desired these two flesh to become one (Genesis 2:24) in marriage to form a family.

Origin | Origin

Every origin story traces back to God and His invisible hand.
An origin contains all future realities embedded within its nature.

God | Invisible hand

Since God created both male and female in His image (Genesis 1:27), He must also contain both within Him.
This is like Eve is found within Adam (Genesis 2:21-22) and all consumption comes from production.

Division | Division

This natural division repeats the extraction process used by God to initially develop Creation.
It can be seen in all areas of life, from cells dividing to a market's division of labor.
It's done in and for the expansion of authentic love, not to start a battle between the sexes.

Adam/Eve | Producer/consumer

Humans were modelled directly after God (Genesis 1:27), starting with Adam.
But God didn't like that Adam was alone (Genesis 2:18), like He was alone before Creation.
So God extracted the rib of Adam to create Eve (Genesis 2:21-22), like consumers come from the rib of producers.

Union | Union

When two complementary beings become one flesh (Genesis 2:24), the outcome is a new creation.

Marriage (family) | Market (free market)

A True Adam and True Eve are to form God's family through marriage.
This is like the producer and the consumer are to bear fruit within a free market.

* * *

God's divide and conquer strategy has a natural harmony if it's able to be embodied.

Economics of Sex

Absolute sex can be extended to economic transactions. The inspiration to extrapolate this came from the series "Laugh Your Way to a Better Marriage" by Mark Gungor.

* * *

There's a sexual cycle embedded within a marriage and market. Each party in the relationship has a unique need designed to be satisfied by the other.

Husband satisfies emotional needs I Entrepreneur satisfies tangible needs

The husband's responsibility is to satisfy his wife's emotional needs. This is like it's the entrepreneur's role to satisfy the customer's tangible need.

Distortion to sex-seeking I Distortion to profit-seeking

Fallen men are dominated by the lust for sex (Genesis 3:6), like fallen producers think only in terms of their own bottom line.

Historical bias of chauvinism I Historical bias of greed

Fallen men have the stereotype of being chauvinistic, like fallen producers are seen as evil or greedy.

Wife satisfies physical needs I Customer satisfies financial needs

The wife's responsibility is to satisfy her husband's physical needs. This is like it's the customer's role to satisfy the entrepreneur's financial needs.

Distortion to emotionally demanding | Distortion to product-demanding

Fallen women are dominated by their manipulative emotions (Genesis 3:1-5), like fallen consumers think only in terms of being materialistically served.

Historical bias as victim | Historical bias as innocent

Fallen women have the stereotype of being the victim, like fallen consumers are seen as helpless or innocent.

Marriages expand love | Markets expand wealth

God's love can expand into a beautiful family and free market if you can enter the cycle of satisfying your spouse's need.

* * *

Absolute sex is the center of Heaven; it's the basis of the entire universe.

Fruits of Love

God made a Garden (Genesis 2:8), not a wild jungle. He has ownership over the Garden via original appropriation, creating the very dust that's mixed with a labor of love (Genesis 2:4-7).

* * *

Every garden takes love to maintain. You have to till the soil, plant and water seeds, prune the plants, pull weeds, harvest the fruit, and do it all over again. That's hard work but it's a natural part of life in the Garden.

Intelligent design | Natural order

Creation had intelligent design (Genesis 1), like the free market has natural order.

Tree of Life (True Adam) | Tree of Life (Producer)

A mature True Adam is the center of the entire Garden with his bride (Genesis 2:9).
He's the son of God who inherits ownership (Genesis 1:29-30), and life itself can bloom because he is the seed of all production.

Tree of Knowledge of Good and Evil (True Eve) | Tree of Knowledge of Good and Evil (Consumer)

A mature Eve knows her inherent choice is when and from whom to accept the seed of production.
Since two become one flesh (Genesis 2:24), everything that Adam owns naturally becomes Eve's property.
Adam and Eve were to have dominion over Creation together (Genesis 1:28), setting the standard of love for their children.

Natural constraints | Natural constraints

The Garden wasn't without but there will always be constraints as long as we're in the physical world.

Divine law/lifespan | Natural law/resources

Divine law (Genesis 2:16-17) and natural laws have constraints to ensure our own well-being.
But there's also a presumption of scarcity considering our physical lifespan or resources like human capital.

Garden of Eden (outside) | Kingdom of Heaven (outside)

Every seed that's not from the Tree of Life is rooted in Satan because of the Fall of Man.

Tree pruning | Political reform

The act of pruning can make the wild olive tree more efficient in its tyranny.
As such, God's primary focus is rebirthing individuals, not limiting the State through political reform.

* * *

Engrafting to the true olive tree (Romans 11:24), Tree of Life, or True Adam eliminates the underlying basis for the State and returns you to a garden with life.

God Bless You

God told Adam and Eve to be fruitful, multiply, and have dominion over Creation (Genesis 1:28). Not only can we can take and apply these blessings to our own life, we can systemize their applicability to the free market.

* * *

A principle that carries through each of the three blessings is the reciprocation of love and beauty as part of natural order.

Fruitful | Fruitful

To be fruitful and to actually bear fruit is to develop yourself as a single entity.

Mind/body | Individual/system(s)

In an individual, the mind loves the body, whose voluntary and involuntary functions carry out and respond in beauty.
This is like an individual producer or consumer reciprocates with systems and processes such as budgets, technologies, or institutions.
A fruitful individual produces a mature sperm or egg, like the development of a market-ready product/service or need.

Multiply | Multiply

To multiply is the combining of two entities which can result in new life.

True Adam/True Eve | Producer/consumer

A True Adam and True Eve both have active participation in the act of marriage.
They each bring to the table the resulting fruit from the previous blessing.
The seed with egg, like product with need, can give birth to a child.

Dominion | Dominion

To have dominion extends love into every facet of Creation, which in return blooms into a beautiful garden.

Family/Creation | Free market/environment

Adam and Eve were to learn, explore, develop, and harvest Creation.
And Creation was designed by God to serve their needs.
This is like free market forces over the natural environment.
The animals, even the institutions, want to reciprocate with the children of God.

Garden of Eden (outside) | Kingdom of Heaven (outside)

You can see the fallen perversion in each blessing when the natural order, for whatever reason, gets reversed.
The body dominates the mind, women dominate men, and the concerns of the environment take priority over mankind.

* * *

We must reject any reversal of this natural order to finally see the blossoming of God's harmonious beauty.

Hero of Trade

You can't consume what you don't first have produced, and God was the very first entrepreneur. He had a desire for joy but was left devastated as the Fall of Man ruined His investment of love. A True Adam continues God's investment strategy by bringing life to where it didn't previously exist.

* * *

An entrepreneur takes the risk, creates employment opportunities, and bears the responsibility. He reaps the fruit of his labor only if he's successful in solving a problem, increasing efficiencies, or otherwise serving a need.

True Adam (husband) I Producer (entrepreneur)

A True Adam and producer are heroic by nature and for what they do.

Means of production I Means of production

A True Adam and producer can spawn through words, sperm, or the means of production.

True Eve (wife) I Consumer (customer)

God didn't like that Adam was alone (Genesis 2:18), and it was only after Eve was created did He say it was very good (Genesis 1:31).
This is like every producer needs a consumer in order to reciprocate in natural order.

True Adam invests love I Producer invests wealth

A True Adam will leave the highest of positions to be with you in the lowest of circumstances.
This is like the investment strategy of "buy low, sell high" which is selling high to go buy low.

Purpose/intent | Purpose/intent

A True Adam seeks to satisfy the needs of True Eve, not strictly his own sexual pleasure.

This is like a producer satisfying consumer needs through value creation, not pursuing profits per se.

The pleasure and profit incentive is a spark that helps start and reinforce the relationship.

Give/take | Supply/demand

A True Adam and True Eve's daily interactions and personal preferences can ebb and flow based on changing desires and market dynamics.

Angels/animals | Employees/institutions

A True Adam doesn't have to delegate to an archangel, employee, or institution.

But, like God in developing Creation, he can create servants (Genesis 1:26) where needed.

* * *

A heroic entrepreneur will do what you'd expect after receiving the beautiful reward of a successful investment – he reinvests.

It Was Very Good

God established a framework of value by saying it was very good (Genesis 1:31).

* * *

Statements like "There are no absolutes." or "Everything is relative." are unsound, illogical, and self-contradicting. In fact, both the absolute and relative exist in harmony.

Absolute value I Absolute value

Absolute value recognizes a moral reality aligned with universal principles.

Relational I Relational

Absolute value manifests when there are two beings within an active relationship.
For instance, a wife makes a man a husband while a husband makes a woman a wife.
This is like a customer establishes the entrepreneur while the entrepreneur establishes the customer.

Divine I Divine

Absolute value stems directly from God.
For instance, every child originates from parents who trace back to Adam and Eve.
Eve came from the rib of Adam (Genesis 2:22), who himself received the breath of life (Genesis 2:7).
This is like all economic actors trace back to an original producer under the invisible hand (Genesis 1:1).
The sheer existence of a moral actor signifies divine value.

Relative value I Relative value

Relative value recognizes the trade-offs between material differences.

Preferential | Preferential

Relative value relies on subjective preferences.
For instance, some families love playing board games, while others are bored playing games.
This is like someone could pay a fortune for what another person would give away for free.

Secondary | Secondary

Relative value supplements absolute value.
For instance, sexual preferences are explored within the context of marriage.
This is like economic preferences exist within moral absolutes.

Garden of Eden (outside) | Kingdom of Heaven (outside)

After the Fall, Adam and Eve became servants to a servant who had relative value.
Humans became a means to an end; to be used or discarded based on utility.
This is like the State uses humanity as a resource to be farmed in the name of progress.

* * *

But the starting point of progress begins with a relationship with God and what He values as good.

Law of the Land

The Garden revolves around God's Word, not a contract with the servant. You cannot expect Adam and Eve to maintain a moral relationship with Lucifer when they couldn't even honor God.

* * *

When God created the universe (Genesis 1), He included a moral framework of natural laws. These laws are already in existence, and we uncover deeper and deeper expressions of their beauty.

Intelligent design | Natural order

There is an intelligent design and natural order to Creation (Genesis 1).
Even the most complicated scenarios are built using simple building blocks.

Divine alignment | Divine alignment

All the laws of nature, including those involving humans, are designed to support healthy relationships.
These laws are honored for the transfer of love and wealth, not for their own sake or for fear of punishment.
The deeper our relationship with God's Word, the greater our natural alignment will reflect order.

Do not eat the fruit | Do not violate natural rights

God warned Adam not to eat the fruit before Eve was even created (Genesis 2:16-17), which made him the moral authority.
The violation of this natural law released death and destruction, not just for Adam and Eve but for their entire family tree (Genesis 2:17).
This is like violating the rights of a single individual has a butterfly effect well beyond just the immediate actors.

One family under God | One nation under invisible hand

When we embody God's Word, written contracts become unnecessary except for basic administration.
There simply would be no incentive to harm our relationship with God or our neighbor (Matthew 22:37-39).

Purpose/intent | Purpose/intent

It's important to start with God's perspective, especially since Satan lied about God's original intent.
God just wanted a family to love, but Satan's lie made it appear that God was holding out on opening their eyes (Genesis 3:1-5).

Ownership | Ownership

A True Adam inherits ownership over Creation (Genesis 1:29-30) and becomes a fulfillment of the law (Matthew 5:17).
His words are the words of God; they are one as he passes this inheritance to you.

Relationships (natural) | Relationships (natural)

The children of God extend their relationship with God into other healthy relationships, including with delegated servants.
The spirit over every relationship and contract would instinctively align with natural law.

Garden of Eden (outside) | Kingdom of Heaven (outside)

Satan's lie changes the spirit, context, and intent of God's Word and law, like the State reinterprets natural laws to further its own agenda.
But no one can override God's Word or laws; we simply choose to ignore the reality of truth.

* * *

A return to natural order involves a relationship with God's Word, the rejection of lies, and a realignment to natural laws.

Let Love Grow

Maturation requires going through various stages of growth.

* * *

The purpose of maturation is to become responsible owners of God's love.

Immature love | Startup wealth

A child, even a baby in the womb, is not evil even though children are completely selfish and ignorant of love.
This is like a startup being selfish in that it requires incoming investment for survival.

Research and development | Research and development

The early stage of a child and start-up are for pure research and development.
They are reliant on others, and their private parts are unproductive by design.

Maturation to marriage | Maturation to market

The transition to adulthood includes accountability over budding sexual desires.
The Fall of Man occurred while Adam and Eve were in the final stages of immaturity.
They had interest to know God's vision (Genesis 3:6), like every startup can't wait to come to market.
But a God-centered marriage, like a market-based solution, takes time to develop.

Time preference | Time preference

The maturation process shifts our viewpoint from a short-term to a long-term perspective.
While you still make short-term decisions, the long-term ramifications are taken into account.

Satan's intervention | State's intervention

A temptation always comes towards the end of the development phase, right as curiosity blooms (Genesis 3:1-5).
These temptations are avoided by abstaining from sex until marriage and then remaining faithful within it.
This is like not accepting State intervention prior to market or once the market is established.

True love | Honest wealth

True love is an active, productive force, not a feeling or materialistic outcome.
This is like honest wealth is measured by the means of production in an economy, not what's in a bank account.

Standard of love | Standard of wealth

A True Adam and True Eve formally establishes God's standard of love and wealth.
This standard is upheld naturally as the cost would be too high for any child to fall.

* * *

You will know the reality of God's love when you experience it firsthand.

Let There Be Light

God produces through the spoken Word (Genesis 1). As the Word is made flesh (John 1:14), Adam follows God by speaking a name to Eve (Genesis 2:23; Genesis 3:20) and producing his divine seed.

* * *

God's love backs the currency underlying all relationships, even economic transactions.

God develops Creation I Invisible hand develops environment

God spoke in an act of production to develop Creation.
He should be recognized as the origin of all production, not the State.
This is like the invisible hand guides the development of the environment.

Eve based on Adam I Consumer based on producer

Eve was created from the rib of Adam (Genesis 2:21-22), like listening is derived from speaking.
This is like every consumer is based on the producer since all consumption comes from the rib of production.

Sexual relationship I Economic transaction

Both participants in the act of marriage are producers to a certain extent.
Adam is a producer but consumes beauty; Eve is a consumer but produces beauty.

Sperm I Product/service

Adam carries the seed of life, like producers generate a product or service.
Adam was God's repository of sperm, like a bank ready to provide honest money.

Egg | Need

Eve's egg was fertilized by the seed, like a consumer's need is satisfied by a product or service.
The reciprocation returns beauty back to Adam, like the payment of money to a producer.

Satan's word | State's fiat currency

A lie from Satan is the distorted production of words (Genesis 3:1-5), like the creation of fiat currency.
Once Satan appropriated Adam's means of production, the entire economy inherits original sin.

Sperm bank | Central bank

A fallen Adam is a sperm bank that produces for Satan using a lifeless seed (Genesis 4:1-2; Genesis 4:25)
This is like a central bank, which is a fallen producer, produces fiat currency for the State.
The means of production isn't just speaking lies; it's reproducing a living, breathing lie.

Marriage distortions | Market distortions

Authentic relationships cannot develop without the whole truth and nothing but the truth.
A lie inserts deceitful words that distort a marriage, like inflation distorts a market.
But a lie can also be the deceitful omission of facts, like artificial deflation in an economy.

* * *

Satan's lies are spoken throughout the very foundation of fallen society. Lies may work at first but they will eventually go bust.

Love and Respect

Love and respect can be extended to economic culture. The inspiration to extrapolate this came from the book "Love and Respect" by Emerson Eggerich.

* * *

There's an energizing cycle of love and respect (Ephesians 5:33) embedded within a marriage and market.

Marriage I Market

Each party in a relationship has a unique need that the other does not have.
Even the biology of sperm and egg reflect this natural dynamic.

Husband I Entrepreneur

The husband needs respect, like the entrepreneur needs respect.
They'll flounder and go out of business without it.

Wife I Customer

The wife needs love, like the customer needs love.
They'll flounder and be depleted without it.

Energizing cycle I Energizing cycle

The unique need is designed to be satisfied by the other.
When this need is satisfied, it reinforces a culture of absolute sex.

Husband -> Wife I Entrepreneur -> Customer

His love motives her respect, like the entrepreneur's love motivates the customer's respect.

Wife -> Husband I Customer -> Entrepreneur

Her respect motivates his love, like the customer's respect motivates the entrepreneur's love.

Lucifer remains servant I Government remains servant

The energizing cycle of a God-centered marriage or market keeps Satan away.

There's no void to try and fill because their love tank is already full.

* * *

Humanity will continue to be in a crazy cycle (Genesis 3:6) until True Adam and True Eve set the standard of love and respect.

Married to Markets

God envisioned the arrangement of Adam with Eve (Genesis 2:18; Genesis 2:22). God wasn't happy with Adam being alone (Genesis 2:18). It was only after creating Eve that God claimed it was very good (Genesis 1:31).

* * *

Marriages are the bedrock of the family, like markets are the basis of the free market.

Marriage I Market

Adam and Eve were to multiply in marriage after being individually fruitful (Genesis 1:28).

Divine law I Natural law

A True Adam and True Eve have a natural respect for laws of God. This is like any codified laws would inherently align with the natural laws in existence.

Family planning I Business planning

God's methods for family planning would naturally have been passed down.
There was intentionality behind the creation of Adam and Eve (Genesis 1:26; Genesis 2:18).
This is like a parental market planning the arise of a downstream market.

Birth of child I Birth of actor

Children are created from the rib of parents, like downstream actors are created from the rib of a developed market.
But not every act of marriage creates a child, like not every economic transaction develops a child actor.

Family | Free market

A true family and free market contains the moral interaction of all participants.

It's not pro-business or pro-women per se, though there will be personal preferences.

Parental forces | Market forces

Parental forces, masculine and feminine, provide structure and support to children.

This is like the market forces providing protection and welfare to the people.

Standard of love | Standard of wealth

A True Adam and True Eve sets the standard of love to be the default pattern.

This is like establishing the standard of wealth in an economy.

There would be no sin, no statism, or even the temptation for fallen love.

Natural elders | Natural elites

There will be natural elders and natural elites as talents are developed.

Their existence is based on their maturation and capacity of love and wealth.

Garden of Eden (outside) | Kingdom of Heaven (outside)

The Fall of Man spawned conflicts of power within marriages and the family.

This is like fallen producers leverage the State to corner the consumer market.

And how fallen consumers leverage the State for premature market production.

Or how children reject natural parental forces in favor of violent rebellion.

* * *

The road to recovery starts within your marriage and your family.

Mine by Right

Adam and Eve were the recipients, embodiments, and owners of God's love. Material ownership extended into the physical world through them. It was their birthright.

* * *

God bequeathed Creation to His children, not to the servant (Genesis 1:29-30), but this inheritance was violated. The misuse of love distorted Adam and Eve's natural right to property, starting with their own flesh and blood.

Garden of Eden (outside) I Kingdom of Heaven (outside)

There is unfortunate baggage inherited because of the Fall of Man.

Satan claims ownership I State claims ownership

Satan claims ownership over our bodies, posterity, and property.
Humanity became reduced to relative value and subjected to the whims of Satan.
This is like the State asserts its ownership over our body and love when any labor or property is taxed or regulated.

Theft of love I Theft of wealth

Satan stole God's property by taking the children and all subsequent material ownership they had been given by God.
The State manifests this theft through the various forms of taxation and regulations.

Double standard I Double standard

Satan stole with the subsequent expectation that his own exercise of property rights be honored.
This is like theft by the State is legitimized while any perceived violation of its property is penalized.

Garden of Eden | Kingdom of Heaven

The principles of ownership can be seen in the underlying relationships of love.

God claims ownership | Invisible hand claims ownership

God and His invisible hand claims ownership over our bodies, posterity, and property.
Humanity was molded out of the dust in order to have a relationship based on love (Genesis 2:7).
This is like the invisible hand claims ownership over our body and love when we offer it back to God.

Transfer of love | Transfer of wealth

The true owner of love is its recipient, though its private property before and after transfer.
True Adam's love is designed to be True Eve's private property.
And True Eve's love is to be owned by True Adam.
This is like a producer's wealth is designed to be the consumer's private property.
And the consumer's wealth is to be owned by the producer.

Universal standard | Universal standard

The actors in a family and free market, including God, respect the right to property.
In doing so, the moral transfer of love and wealth is able to flow where mutually desired.

* * *

There's a direct connection between the first principles of unadulterated love and the exchange of property.

Name the Animal

God created through the Word but leaves part of the process to us, making us co-creators. Adam was responsible for naming the animals (Genesis 2:19-20), and even God was curious to see what would happen (Genesis 2:19-20).

* * *

Animals are like angels, employees, or the institutions of man. They are servants.

God creates angels I Producer creates employees

God created the angels, including powerful archangels.
This is like a producer creates employees, including powerful institutions.

Delegated responsibility I Delegated responsibility

Angels, like employees, have authority delegated to them by their owner.
But owners can only transfer responsibility able to be delegated within natural law.
For instance, if you can't steal from your neighbor, you can't delegate that action either.

Capacity to choose I Capacity to choose

Angels, like animals, must have some capacity of choice, otherwise the Fall of Man couldn't occur.
This is like employees and institutions must also have choice in relation to carrying out their duties.

Designed to serve I Designed to serve

Every angel or animal is intended to serve a purpose that's defined by its owner.
This is like humans enter into the servant role by accepting a position of employment.

Employees voluntarily agree to the owner's terms of employment to serve as designed.

Ownership I Ownership

Adam inherits ownership simply by being the son of God (Genesis 1:29-30).
He is to align himself with God's Word and natural laws, not the policies of Lucifer or civil laws per se.

Nullification I Nullification

The right of ownership inherently includes the capacity to reject consent.
Adam can negate, even override the decisions made by the servants.
This is like the people can directly nullify or void civil laws passed by politicians.

Angels/animals I Employees/institutions

Adam's ownership includes the authority over servants (Genesis 1:29-30).
This necessarily includes naming an animal for dinner, clothing, or experimentation.
This is like eliminating a job role or abolishing an entire institution.

Self-defense I Self-defense

The right of self-defense exists against servants and humans.

Against servants, Adam conceivably has the right to eliminate Lucifer, but he certainly had the right defend against Satan.
Animals, like the snake in the Garden, can become violent and may need to be put down.
This is like firing an abusive employee or defending against a predatory institution.

Against humans, the right to self-defense protects against demonic men.

These violent individuals effectively become worse than animals in nature.

* * *

Within the borders of an unadulterated Garden of Eden, you don't need to exercise self-defense, at least not against your fellow man. But wild animals and misunderstood natural laws can still to be found at the unexplored edges of the Garden.

Price of Admission

Prices coordinate human action in conversation, sex, and economic transactions. There's an ebb and flow between the give and take of finite resources. These complementary, not contradictory, forces are built into God's design of every relationship.

* * *

A relationship finds an equilibrium when both the supply and demand forces unite for an exchange. There's stability in this process when not distorted by the State.

Marriage signals | Market signals

A marriage and market use signals for conveying information.

Proposition discovery | Price discovery

The initial part of any marriage is getting to know the cues of your spouse.
This is like price discovery supporting the integration of a product into market.

Natural vitality | Honest profit

A beautiful response received from the successful transfer of love contains vitality.
This is like part of the revenue received from a successful investment contains profit.
These signals become powerful incentives to continue in an energizing cycle.

Natural constraints | Natural constraints

We live in a finite world where natural constraints exist.
Verbal propositions are subject to the physical constraints of your voice.
For instance, speaking too loudly isn't sustainable and speaking too softly may fail to convey the message.

This is like pricing signals are subject to the natural constraints of the market.
For instance, the cure to high prices is high prices and the cure for low prices is low prices.

Satan's intervention I State's intervention

Satan offers a cheaper, immoral price that deceitfully hides the true cost.
The signals are distorted by and redirected to benefit the State.

Reduced price I Reduced price

Adam and Eve's fallen sex came at a reduced price, namely not requiring God's approval.
But, like spoken lies, free sex isn't free even though its price appears cheaper upfront.
This is like the State appears altruistic by subsidizing part of economy to reduce prices.
But this coercively distorts the market forces and will always result in a higher long-term cost.

Higher cost I Higher cost

Adam and Eve felt the unexpected burden of cursed grounds (Genesis 3:17) and painful labor (Genesis 3:16), which is a cost that continues to be paid by posterity.
This is like the loss of productivity and the extra burden of compliance is a higher cost felt by current and future actors.
The long-term cost of accepting illicit intervention is nothing short of self-destruction, like the collapse of your own economy.

* * *

There's no greater distortion of signals than those related to marriage and markets. We must release these signals from demonic forces in order to see the beauty God envisioned.

Rock of Truth

The gold being good (Genesis 2:11-12) foreshadows its role as money.

* * *

A producer first delivers gold as a product to satisfy the consumer's need. The gold is later returned as honest money to satisfy the producer's need.

God's Word | Invisible hand's money

God's Word forms the basis and standard for moral transactions (Genesis 2).

Store of value (truth) | Store of value (gold)

God's Word is valuable since it's based on eternal truths.
This is like money throughout history held its value when based on gold.

Medium of exchange (language) | Medium of exchange (currency)

Even though truth and gold directly act as a means of transfer (John 14:6), their exchange is often through a language or currency.
Languages evolve over time as new words are added and others are lost in the pursuit of truth.
This is like currencies have natural adjustments in relation to the reality of gold.

Unit of account (definition) | Unit of account (measure)

The unit of account sets the standard through which to define or measure value.
God's Word sets the definition of truth through which to judge good and evil.
This is like revealing the lies of fiat currency through the prism of gold.

Satan's word | State's fiat currency

Satan's word forms the basis and standard for immoral transactions (Genesis 3:1-5).

Store of value (lie) | Store of value (fiat)

Satan's word is not valuable since it's based on an underlying deception.
This is like the State's monetary policy is based on the fraudulent credit of a fiat currency.

Medium of exchange (language) | Medium of exchange (currency)

Satan and the State ensure a functioning means of communication and exchange.
They need it in order to carry out their own demonic interests.

Unit of account (definition) | Unit of account (measure)

Satan imposes an alternate unit of account by redefining what truth is.
This is like the State imposing its fiat currency through legal tender laws.
These coercive distortions remove God's Word and honest money from circulation.

* * *

When we become the embodiment of truth, we are the living word returning beauty back to God. Our spoken will would also be God's will, but to get there means putting your money where your mouth is.

School of Love

The family is the school of love. It's the place where love was first destroyed (Genesis 3:6), and it'll be the place where love is restored.

* * *

The family and free market can be broken down into four core relationships, two vertical and two horizontal in nature.

Husband <-> Wife | Entrepreneur <-> Customer

A husband and wife's intimate relationship is the engine that creates new life.
This is like market romance between an entrepreneur and customer develops new actors.

Parent -> Child | Market actor -> Child actor

Parents have the blessing to raise children, like a parental market raises downstream actors.
These children can themselves be coming to market or already established in marriage.

Child -> Parent | Child actor -> Market actor

The relationship of a child towards parents is like a downstream actor towards its market of origin.
Children cannot choose their parents, even in rebirth situations, but you can come to know their sacrifice and investment.
It's the wisdom of a maturing child to come to understand and reciprocate honor to the generation(s) who came before.

Sibling <-> Sibling | Peer <-> Peer

Sibling love is between those who share the same parents, like between peers under the same market.
They each have their own relationship to an upstream market as they mature to or within their own market.

Each actor is secure in their own identity and receipt of parental love, so any rivalry spurs further productivity.

* * *

The family is the school where the individual learns to serve a higher purpose and the collective supports every individual to bloom into their God-given potential. It's the place where love and wealth is accumulated.

Tree of Liberty

The family is an institution created directly by God. God wanted Adam and Eve to multiply (Genesis 1:28) into an ever-expanding network of families.

* * *

The free market is a market of families; all stemming from a True Adam.

Adam -> Family I Producer -> Free market

An individual, starting with Adam, is the smallest minority.
And a married couple, like Adam and Eve, becomes the smallest collective.
This is like an individual producer within a collective market.
These collectives culminate into a family and free market.

Division of labor I Division of labor

There's a natural division of labor where individuals specialize in areas where they are divinely unique.
Every contribution of God-given talent showcases inequality as a beautiful feature of the family.

Divine identity I Divine identity

A true identity isn't provided by or trapped within a particular archangelic framework.
It's based on familial or free market relationships, ultimately being a child of God.

Collective reinforcement I Collective reinforcement

The collective set of individuals respect the natural rights of each and every family member.
The free market, like the family, culturally reinforces the value of the individual.

Family characteristics | Free market characteristics

There are natural characteristics of the family and free market.

Multi-dimensional | Multi-dimensional

Families are a multi-dimensional set of interrelated relationships.
There are vertical relationships and horizontal relationships.
And there is the whole extended family in indirect free market relationships.

Multi-generational | Multi-generational

There are individuals at every stage of life within a family.
Every generation gives way to a new generation as older markets fade and new ones develop.

Lineage hierarchy | Lineage hierarchy

The family is based on blood, not meritocracy like employment or institutions.
Each branch of the family tree traces back to God, not the servant.

Garden of Eden (outside) | Kingdom of Heaven (outside)

Satan captured Adam's means of production to distort the entire family tree.
His children are disconnected from the lineage of God and their value is reduced to mere relative, meritocratic values.
And the hierarchy of competency favors those most skilled in deceit and gathering conformity to the State's agenda.

* * *

A free market is just a natural extension of God's family. And the focus is on family relationships, not servant institutions.